All the
Beginnings
of
Everything

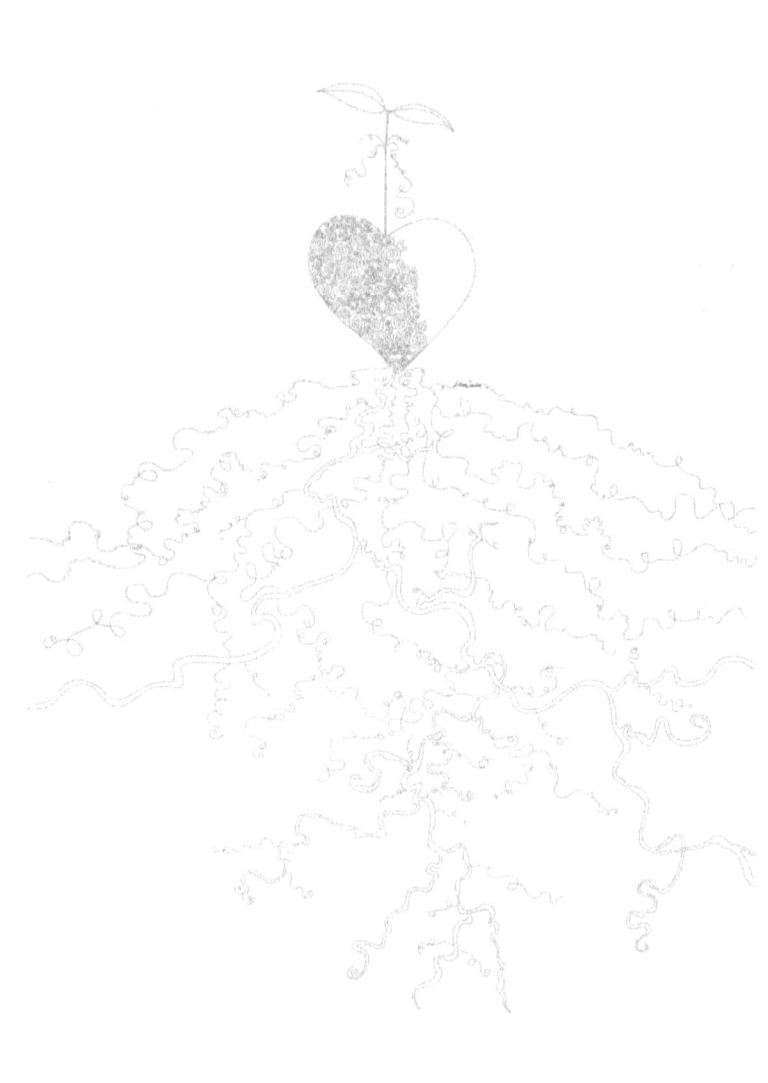

**Praise for
All the
Beginnings
of
Everything**

Austin has, yet again, created a masterpiece. *All the Beginnings of Everything* is a sensational collection which spans what feels like a lifetime. Separated into seven parts, Austin explores more in this collection than I feel she ever has done before, without sacrificing her trademark style. Her words remain sharp, raw and honest.

Part one is succinct, fervent and reveals how our childhoods fall into our adult years, no matter how hard we try to leave the past in the past. This is followed by parts two and three: Austin's ode to self and survival. She is the lioness empowered by her dismissal of those who tried to break her. She will not give thanks; she is the reason she is here today and she will continue to create her own light and legacy.

For me, part four was a departure for Austin. Although she explores grief as masterfully as she did in *Constant Muses* and *TWELVE*, here Austin also embraces hope. It is an honest account of how heartache demolished the walls of her heart in order to help rebuild them, stronger than before. This balance of loss and love is repeated in parts five and six as we journey through hurt, lust, unrequited love and goodbyes to find real love; love which feels like a Heaven-sent gift and the easiest thing in the world.
Finally, fittingly, part seven delivers the end of this collection and takes us back to the beginning. This part is

Austin through and through; it holds some of the best pieces I believe she has ever written. The title poem is quite simply, a masterpiece.

With each new release, Austin's craft continues to blossom and out-do what came before. I cannot describe her words and work in any other way than magic. Not because her words appear as if by magic but because she wields a power many would struggle to harness. She is true; and for that, in this day and age, she is otherworldly.

—Kristiana Reed, *Between the Trees*

Kindra M. Austin's new collection is a masterstroke that makes all of her previous collections pale in comparison. Intense, melancholic and at once, encapsulating love; Austin's journey comes full circle. If you were moved by the grief and self-deprecation of Constant Muses and TWELVE, the power behind her voice is no less powerful, but wiser. The entire book is testament to the strength of a feminine spirit this world cannot entice to stay quiet.

For that, we are all better off.

—Nicholas Gagnier, *The Olivia and Hale series*

Books
written by
Kindra M. Austin

poetry

> Constant Muses
> TWELVE

fiction

> Magpie in August
> For You, Rowena

All the
Beginnings
of
Everything

by Kindra M. Austin

All the Beginnings of Everything
© 2019 Kindra M. Austin

Cover design and illustration by Allane Sinclair

Editor: Christine E. Ray
Consultant: Candice Louisa Daquin

All rights reserved.
Printed in the United States of America.

No part of this book may be used, stored in a system retrieval system, or transmitted, in any form or in any means—by electronic, mechanical, photocopying, recording, or reproduced in any manner whatsoever—without written permission from the author, except in the case of brief quotations embodied in critical articles and reviews.

For information, address Indie Blu(e) Publishing.
indieblucollective@gmail.com

Published in the United States of America by Indie Blu(e) Publishing.

ISBN: 978-1-7328000-9-0
Library of Congress Control Number: 2019946937

Dedication

For the girl
I once was,
and the woman
I've
become,
because of all
the shit
I got.

For Nicole,
my baby girl—
everything
began with you.

For my sister,
Tara,
the hair twirler.

For Mom,
always.

Foreword
by Candice Louisa Daquin

All the Beginnings of Everything is a *tour du force*, one woman carrying the kaleidoscope of her family tree. In many ways, phantasmagoric in its debt to allegory, metaphor, and visceral self-talk. It's a world outside of time, revealing how everything started and the patterns we never see tattooed beneath our skin, multiplying with every choice. All beg the questions, what is fate, and what is within our control? Can we save ourselves and others from prior outcomes? Will the tapestry of our ancestors dictate our own destiny, irrespective of our effort to be free?

If you have ever lost someone very dear to you, did you expect a mere year to heal that loss? Of course not. Yet in our world of social immediacy, the flip side is a subtle intolerance to any difficult enduring emotion. Perhaps because of that, as well as the necessary value of undying love and recognition of loss, a book written after the initial fallout of Austin losing her mother, has a reflective depth that is redolent with the exquisite emotional tapestry we know her formidably capable of.

Personally, I have long appreciated the method of poetry Austin bleeds, which ends without ending, as if about to say something else and then choosing not to. It leaves you eternally with a question, a longing for the next thought, a capricious, honest, realistic response to emotions that are never neatly packaged.

It takes someone whose wrestling with language is so in-tune as to be able to present something unfinished that has as much value as a more self-conscious neat beginning, middle and end. As if we're stepping into Austin's head rather than her pen, as if we have gotten closer than is possible, clawing through the satellites orbiting around her blaze.

For those of us who read *Constant Muses* and then *Twelve*, the trajectory of loss, and conversely, its accompanying poetic beauty, are familiar totems in Austin's life. Though the young indie author may have devoted her focus on this loss, as any would, there is between the cracks so much more to behold. At the same time, if that were all there were, it would be enough because like any cast of characters, living or passed on, we begin to care and attach ourselves to Austin's people. We get inside their heads via her ability as an author to convey alternate universes.

There is a palpable feeling of loss and grief but also an accompanying idea of inheritance and personhood. Who are we when we lose our mothers? Who are we as mothers? Who are we as sisters? Will those we love inherit or be injured by the same set of genes that began the pain in the first place? "Now, I smile/when you think that/I should be ashamed." (I've Just Got the Hang of It Now).

Questions many of us ask but never aloud, are fearlessly queried in the fast-growing climbing ivy that is the white fire of Austin's clever brain. She's faced the worst pain and now she can be as fearless as any human being can be, given they are subject to the whim of an unknown world.

You couldn't if you tried, categorize Austin's 'style.' Not because she doesn't have any, she almost gleams with it, but because she's already danced away from the little box you were going to put her in before shocking you with another tongue. There's something infinitely unpredictable and erotic about an unapologetic, hot-under-the-collar female writer who takes no prisoners; "I've defiled my own name." (Slick).

Austin knows how much spice to add and swims between the blatantly sensual to the darkest coves, and then out into the light where she exposes her truths. Her voice doesn't remain the same, there's obvious influences, but she's all things, the female Bukowski, the smart Joan Didion, then Tennyson takes over and gets epic. It never gets staid. Austin is a writer you want to befriend and talk to all night long over many drinks. You feel you'd find the riddle to the universe if you survived it.

I hope you will relish Austin's latest collection of mostly unpublished work that is as new as it is ancient and venerated by the depths she is willing to go to convey her existence, and validate the right we all have to exist in many moods. You won't be able to look away. Not for an instant. She's the kind of girl we're all wanting to be when we pick up a pen and wonder why we can't just spill blood on the page.

—Candice Louisa Daquin, *Pinch the Lock*

Thank You

Christine E. Ray; my mentor, partner, editor, and Kirk to my Spock. Our connection is deep and true, and you, my friend, keep me sane. I love you like crazy. Thank you!

Candice Louisa Daquin; yours is a writing talent unsurpassed. You're a sister in wordsmithing and advocacy. I admire you, and love you endlessly. Thank you for your undying support, loving heart, and friendship.

Nicole Lyons; you're my forever lioness, and an inspiration to me in all you do as a human being, a writer and a mental health advocate. You are truth, and I love you. Thank you for always encouraging me.

Allane Sinclair; I've been loving you so long, you're weaved into the fabric of my being. I could write a book about our epic friendship. I think I will one day, because everyone should know what a beautiful, talented, and genuine human being you are, every day, without question. Thank you for everything.

Table of Contents

part I
on Family, Here and Elsewhere   **1**

part II
on the Metaphysical   **27**

part III
on the Depraved   **43**

part IV
on Salvation   **59**

part V
on Bad Love   **79**

part VI
on Love-Love   **105**

part VII
on My Ever Changing State of Mind   **115**

part I
on Family, Here and Elsewhere

**She Twirls Her Hair
With Mad
Dexterity**

A habit formed in utero,
she twirls her hair
with mad
dexterity—

    knots untying knots untying knots untying...

A habit formed in utero,
she twirls her hair
with mad
dexterity,
just like our mother had.

And when I watch my little sister
tie
and untie
her dark silk,
I am comforted;

For she,
at least,
inherited something—

    knots untying knots untying knots untying...

Sister

I

Sister hides
behind
brunette mantle
painted
burgundy;
and I wonder
whether
obscured amber orbs
jammed inside her eye
sockets
are human,
or glass
beads that once belonged
to her favorite baby
doll.

II

Sister says,
I'm cursed like Mother,
and I wonder
whether
she owns vocal
cords,
or plastic
baby
mama box
manufactured
in Japan.

If I shake her,
will she speak
faster?

Awful lot of questions
Sister won't answer,
unprovoked.

III

Sister says,
Love me harder.
Please,
don't let me go.

And I know
that I could
never
watch my
little
girl
blow.

He Speaks In Mysteries

Someday
baby,
you're gonna
understand
that what you know now,
is not exactly what you
knew.

You've gotta
ask yourself,
see:
*what does this person want
from me?*

You've gotta be smarter—
gotta pay attention.

Because if you're smarter,
and
you pay attention,
you can
convince them

That what they'd thought they wanted
was
never
what they'd
wanted
in the first goddamn place.

Do you get what I'm saying?

                                    Yes, Daddy. I think so.

How old are you?

                                                I'm seven.

Then behave like you're seven.
You're not a goddamn dummy.

                                  No, I'm not a dummy.
                                    I love you, Daddy.

I love you, too, baby.

Red Paint and Beach Sand

I

In the kitchen,
my mother was dead with no religion.
She'd bumped her head,
and painted the floor.

Dead head,
red
linoleum.

Mama,
were your eyes closed or open?
Only
tabby cat knows.

II

Bloated
bag of bones,
spoiling
organs, and skin
leaking;

You
wasted
away for six nights
and
seven days.

III

Now you're drained and
taking space
in stainless
steel
chest of drawers.

You don't belong there.

You were our
lioness.
Goddamned alcoholic,
but lioness, nonetheless.

IV

It happened.

You've been made
into
ashes.

Furious furnace,
not
as furious as
me.

Pulverized bones
resemble precious
beach
sand in Tawas,
fittingly.

V

Pour your
bits into silver
vessel.

Hang you
'round our weeping necks.

A talisman.

VI

No one can hurt you now.
Not your mother
or your father.
Not corrupt Jehovah—
backhanded god,
cruel lesson maker.

VII

My mother is dead.
And it doesn't fucking
matter
whether
her eyes
were closed or open.

Those eyes
I'll never see again;
most brilliant
that beheld me the day I was born.

The ones
made dull when
she bumped her head,
and
painted the floor.

**You're Missing
the
Point**

Jehovah is King—

You don't
have the
room to spare
inside your
malnourished
heart.

Jehovah is King—

His name
is sour
on
my
tongue; and

I wish you'd gag
on testaments
you blindly
recite.

Jehovah is King—

You sold him
your soul
at the cost of
your daughter,
my mother.

Jehovah is King—

You're missing
the
point.
You are
not
Christian.
I
will not
mourn you.

I'm happy I have your potato salad recipe.

**Get Gone,
Goss'mer
Mama**

Up
and away,
I watch you
go—

Get gone,
goss'mer
mama,

On
an autumn day.

You are
spider
fibers,

Unweaving
in the breeze.

Do not cry
for me down here,

When you see me
eating
dirt—

Earth that
you
once

walked
upon;

I
will savor flavors,
in
memoriam.

All That Remains Is Everything

All that remains is
everything

I have—

Peace
on my mind,
steel
shielded veins,
and
love
inside my heart.

But Everything
I have
just isn't
fucking
good
enough.

Because

All that remains is
everything

Mom
and Auntie had,
when they
lived.

And
there will never
be anything
more than
everything,
now.

**Itching
My
Soul**

All
gone
suddenly, swallowed
by
big
nothing.

I've buried them
within
the layers of
my
skin.

The women
I'd
adored—

Red soaked
wool
itching
my
soul.
Maddened,
I
scratch

The pestilence
that festers
too

beautifully
to quit.
No,
I cannot
quit.

These scars are
proof
they existed.

**For the Women
I've Lost**

Nothing
scares me here.

I've built my house
around
those who haunt me.

Bone brick and
crimson mortar
rises tall—a keep.

The older I grow, so
does my fortress.

I'd like to be
left alone
to revel
in my ghosts in
peace.

I'd like to be
left alone,
where I belong—

Serenity of
solitude.

For then I
would be
happy

in spite of
all this
mourning.

Soon,
I know,
I'll hold them.

And we will
weigh the
same.

Soon,
I'll throw a
party
for the women
I've lost

Inside this
goddamed
house I've
built.

**I Still Have Your
Goddamn Glass Bowl**

I want to know
you're home
without
making a phone
call.

I haven't called enough;
seen you
enough,
hugged you
enough.

I want to
tell you
something
funny
because
I miss
the sound of
your laughter.

I just want
you to be here;
within this
fucked up
gravity
where
I exist,
out
in the garage,

smoking Basic cigarettes.

I know where you
lived,
and I want to
come visit.

I still have your
goddamn glass bowl.

**I'm Sorry I Don't
Miss You
More**

I (think) I
know
too much
about you.

No, I do not
miss
you,
just
some things
I *remember*
about you:

Crisp
eyes loud with love
for me,
and

The way you'd
tease
when we'd
play
restaurant.

I tried to be a
good
waitress,
but you
were a terrible
customer.

I'm sorry I don't
miss you
more.

And I'm sorry
that I didn't
see you
through your
cancer.

**The
Fatal**

Bald,
and fragile—

Crooked body bloated
with poison
to fight the
fatal
that was
killing you.

I should have
said,
    I love you.

Instead,
I said,
    Good to see you.

part II
on the Metaphysical

**Welcome
To the
Strange**

Welcome
to the
strange
state
of estrangement
from permafrosted
anguish
and
inimical sentiment

**Of the
Stars**

Of the
stars
we are born;

And to the
stars
we shall return

As dust
welcomed
home,

If you
so
believe.

**Don't Forget To
Play
The Turtles**

Happy Together

Yes,
my girl,
we have
been.

Don't forget to
play
The Turtles—

Call me,
and I'll come with
visions
of us
jumping
on the bed and singing
our
second love song.

All Gone, Totally

Energy
can neither be
created
nor
destroyed.

I am, and

I
will
not
be.

My mind
will transcend
both space
and
time;

And
I will
be
transformed,

Like mother and father,
and
all
our
ancestors.

I cannot be all
gone,

Totally.

And so I do not
fear my death—

Only the loneliness
left in my stead.

On the Flip-Side

My loved
ones do
live
in the breezes
of

Some
place,

'Neath
golden
apple skies,
and

Among
those fields of
heather

Every-
one
excites about.

Yes,
in the breezes
on the

Flip-Side,

My loved ones
drink honey

and dine on
ambrosia
while I
fill my
gut with ashes,
unconsecrated.

**I've Designed My
Afterlife
Estate**

I've designed my
afterlife

Estate—

Blueprints
drawn up
on my
heart.

Oaks and
maples and
corpulent
evergreens
and grapevines and wizened
crab-apple trees on three acres with
a hill out back and an algae green swamp
at the landing before the dense woods where
my cat Thomas ran and never came in for dinner.

Green house with
a bay window made for
massive Christmas trees and a
sunroom that kept an absurd surplus of
toys and once was haunted but the spirit was
evacuated by a bible my parents didn't believe in
and our Jehovah's Witness neighbor named Nelson.

I've designed my afterlife estate.

Blueprints drawn up on my heart
when I was seven and grew up fast
beneath the boulder of domestic
abuse.

Why would I want to
recreate that place?

Because it was a
critical ingredient
in the
recipe of me.

**And Nearly
Must Be Good
Enough**

Here I am,
gliding
through the
In Between—

I captain
my ship
full
sail,
flitting

Inside
eye-blinks
just
to
glimpse
you,

Darling girl
with golden
hair.

You can nearly
see me
see you
with your
steel blue
eyes.

And nearly
must be good
enough,

Because

Your petal lips,
      (formed in my womb)
peel gently back for
white teeth
I have
always
adored.

I Will Live Forever If I Damn Well Want To

And
I do
want to
live
forever

Through my
words
written

I
am a
goddess
of
creation

Through my
words
written

I've
been
granted
immortality

Through my
words
written

Some-
one will
always
remember
me

Through my
words
written

**And If
I'm Called to Live
Another Earthly
Life**

When I forget
this given name
and made to
learn a new one,

I will
remember
you,

Even if I be
a tree
and live one thousand years.

part III
on the Depraved

Jacket Tossed Over My Lap

Your searching
fingers
pierced me.
I bit my bottom
lip;
worried I would
bleed
enough
for you to notice.
I made a noise,
mistaken,
and you kissed my ear
with wet tongue.
You said I was beautiful
amongst your friends
who smiled
high,
in the loop.
And when we parked,
I begged,
please don't,
but you did
get off
thrusting
hard between my breasts
squeezed,
a consolation prize.
The least I owed
for being
a fucking cock tease.

I Was Your Good Bitch

    Snap my back,
    and
    crack my limbs
    against your knee.

I would let you
break my bones
and bend me into

Inhuman
shapes
you
preferred.

    Fold me.
    Drag me.
    Undo me.
    Fuck me.

Your
beloved
bloody
contortionist;

Teeth
clenched sticks,
doggy-style.

You had me trained
to embrace

dysfunction.

I was your good
bitch.

Bellyful
(a revision)

Excuse
my protrusion;

I suffer
intrusion
of demons mine, and yours

Forced
between my
teeth.

I masticate
while you
masturbate,

Fun to watch me
swallow,
innit?

Pour a stiff drink,
something acetic
acid—

Make
my stomach
into plastic
lined landfill,

Non-
biodegradable.

I'm gonna
die
bloated with a bellyful
of demons, yours and mine,
worm-like and
immortal.

Slick

Running on midnight,
oil
peels 'neath
my flit feet—
heel to toe,
heel to toe; but
toil and tarry with nary a mile
made distant.

Sluts like me
are
always found out,
cos spouses see the
webs of deceit
weaved with widow-like legs
wide open—
not as stupid as we
pretend. Oh!

We do pretend
our husbands' best friends,
or
brothers-in-law,
or
bosses all
have hearts
appended
to their throbbing dicks.

"And that dick's heart beats only for me."
(Swoon!)

Slut found out

living in a small town,
sucking on
spoils—

I'm gonna fucking die here,
defamed.

I've
defiled
my own
name.

Sex Without a Heard Affirmative

Promiscuity,
present
or
past

Sayin no
now,
when at first
they said
yes

Out
all night,
gettin fuckin
blotto

Strippin
for
a
livin

None of it fuckin
matters

Sex without
a
heard
affirmative

Is
>   rape

Is
>   rape

Is
>   rape

Is
>   rape

Is
>   rape

Is
>   rape

Is
>   rape

Is
>   rape

Is
>   rape

Is
>   rape

Is
>   rape

Because I'm a Whore
Who Asked For It
(a revision)

I quite like the dark side, dear.
Show
me your shadows,
those
phallic phalanges,
and feel up
my female.

I quite like the fusty spoors
of spirits,
and semen,
and plundered
blood

Smeared
upon
my plastic skin.

I quite like
the emptiness

Settled
in the pit of me—

The sharp taste
on my tongue
as I lick
the edge of
abyss

While you
excuse
on evening news.

Dehumanize
me.

Because I'm a whore
who asked for it,

Simply
by breathing.

For Your Consideration

Clothing
and alcohol/
drug
consumption
are all
irrelevant

When it really comes
down to
the reasons a
shit-bag
rapist
rapes.

Victim blamers,
for your
consideration:

Shut the fuck up,
or get a goddamned clue.
All you do
is discourage the reporting
of sexual assault
and instigate
further
emotional
damage.

Making a Killing

Making money hand over trigger—
gotta get that paper if
you wanna be a Christian
Gangster.
Seeds of Judas the quick silver taker
prey;
tell me what it feels like living in lined pants, and
I will oblige you with my medical bills.
You deserve a laugh,
after all, it must be awfully
grueling
strategizing behind our backs—
making money hand over fists
full of pills that we can ill afford
while you all enjoy those orgies with
insurance companies.
Tell me what it feels like to come in the
faces of the dying.

**Political
Machine**

Mechanically separated
human meat freaks,
reformed.

part IV
on Salvation

**I Snake
East**

The pit of me bleeds;
sins
pooling in my feet,
and eating
upward,

Resettle
in the gut that
I've abused
with lies and liquor
and egoism.

Before me stretch two
paths:

March heavy west
toward
Perdition,
or onward east
to seek
Redemption.

I drag my legs behind me;
on my belly
I snake
east.

**Underwent
a
Metamorphosis**

Asked
my
reflection,

> *Who are you?*
> *You look familiar,*
>   *like an old friend.*

Answered
I
with mouth
of flesh,

> "I'm no one to you,
>   let's not pretend."

How About Those Hotdogs?

The ones I'd left defrosting
for you
on the kitchen counter

After
I accepted who you are
and realized
who the
fuck
I
am,

And walked out the door
with dignity—

My dignity.

You'd tried
to keep it
hidden.

Thank you for aiding
in the salvation
of me.

And They Will Paint Her No More

They painted her
violent
shades
of sovereignty.

Topography
of kingdumbs—

Mountains
and chasms
were marked
on her skin.

And she did
begin
to call their
purple
sins
her own—

Poorly
princess
of cesspit
love.

And the court
were all
certain
they'd buried
her mettle.

They held festival
to celebrate their
conquer,

But the
great beast
who lived inside her
said never
to settle.

So she dug a hollow
into the earth,
and there
she did nurture
the dragon heart
growing,
and bowing her rib cage.

Now she is
emerged with steel shielded
veins.

And they will paint her
no more.

Re:
For All the Shit I Got

Dear_____,

I have been alive,
more often than I've not;

And there's something to be said,
for all the shit I got—

Interventions,
undivine
undermined
my best intent,

And

So I be
misunderstood,

Unliving
for no greater good,
for all the shit I got.

For all the shit I got—

I do naught
but pray to
you,
and
you say:

Dear_____,

Speak not my name,
and claim
your own,

For all the shit you got.

Great White Wing

I sense your presence best in dark,
impalpable;
when eyes, mine
cannot see.
But I can smell
sweet milk
cleaving to your breath.

And hearken—
your lungs
speak
in tongues,
tailored
for my despairing.

I build fortresses
formed from unbleached
bones of so many
rib cages
made unnecessary.
Damn Death,
and His scythe.

And hearken—
your lungs
speak
in tongues,
tailored
for my despairing.

I sense your presence best in dark;
Great White
Wing
of Hope,
alive inside my
rib cage
still necessary,
you carry me to the sun.

Gather
golden fire;
raze my lifeless
weary,
time
and time again.

**Jesus and the
Wolves**
(a revision)

Amazing Grace! How deaf—
silence,

Wet wool wrapped
'round
my head.

I've been saved, but not by you.
Jesus
is just alright.

Won't sleep over;

He complains
of bellyaches and
always
flies home
early.

Maybe my snacks are too bitter
tasting.
I've given up sweet wine.

My blessings are colored
black and blue;

They come with
the taste of

dirt,
and the blood of
gnashing teeth.

My blessings
sing

Like a choir of
wolves
alive
inside
my rib cage.

I have saved myself.

**I've Got
the Hang of It
Now**

Now,
I
applaud

After something
true
I've said;

Now,
I
smile

When you think that
I
should
be

Ashamed
for having
the
audacity

To cast
off
the
blame
that you've projected
onto me.

Funny thing is,
I'm not angry
        (much).

It's just that
I've got
the hang of it
now.

**I Was Salvageable
After All**

And I'm
better than good without
your

Discernment, and
backhanded compliments.

Better than good without
your

Vomit in my hair, and the taste of
your
authority in my mouth.

And I'm so much fucking
better than good
without your

Lying teeth clenched on
my integrity.

See?
I was salvageable
after all.

Selene, Titan Deity

Mother Moon,
usher of diamond dust,

I am cleansed.

**Shield
Maiden**

The fire that whelms me does
not consume;
for it is mine
own—

I do
control
inferno,

A blood-borne lust to
conquer
pain.

Here you come with
buckets of water,

And a head
distended
with ego,

Convinced
that I'm
a woman in
distress.

The fire that whelms me does
not consume;
for it is mine
own—

My
defense
mechanism,

Desire to live
forged in
flame.

Deliverance

You are love letters sent
over landscapes and seas
underneath the heavens.

Abounding
radiance
eclipses my obscurity.

Lo lamenting heart
o' mine—

Violence
eviscerated by
deliverance.

part V
on Bad Love

I Meant It Metaphorically

I said I'd be your wings,
so you hired a flat-felled seamstress
who
topstitched me to your back.

Save me, you say
when jumping off bridges.

**Of
Fairytales**

Tarnished fairy tales—

Playwrights
tragedians
star-crossed nothing
but sky.

Moonlight paints you
angel white and me
the daemon.

Stonewashed dogma—

Canon locked
and loaded.

Peace be with you.

Speeding

Two fucking selfish—

You were worth the heartbrake
applied,
halting impeding
wreck.

**Like
Autumn Leaves**

He is the rain on a cold grey day—
the arthritis that ravages my bones,
and when he breathes,
it's a Nor'easter wind.

I'm blown apart;
shattered;
scattered;
kicked about like
autumn leaves,
dead.

The Moon Is a Phantasm—
a Projection of You

Your cold white face casts shadows
of me against these cobblestone streets
and up the sides of Tudor buildings.

I am a colossus
in spite of you.

You Were No Atheist

I found a photo of us,
eight years old,
stored in my 'sent messages.'
We're sat at Tokyo
smoking a cigarillo,
looking utterly chuffed with ourselves.

I thought I had destroyed all
evidence
of the Archer and the
Scorpion union.

God*damn*, darling, we made a
fucking stunning
couple when we
stepped out dressed in gangster black,
and with a dirty
day drink buzz-on.

But we were
stunninger
in the dark,
when you worshipped
at Church of Me;
your platform bed served well
as altar.
2 a.m. moon soaked Liturgy,
my sweet heathen,
you were no atheist
sheathed in my silk.

**Dilly Dalliance
Bound Me**

Lavender dipped
indulgent tongue
dripped incantations,
salacious songs—
your abuse was tender

Dilly dalliance
bound me
with feathers

**I Feel
Confident**

I'm trimming those
frayed ends,
and
sharpening
those
pointy convictions—

Giving
them a sharp edge,
a serrated opinion,

Ready to pierce you
where it hurts more.

A Murder Amongst Roses

My heart
doth bleed to death
sweetly
and petal soft—

A murder amongst
roses.

Lay me down, and keep me down
selfishly
in petal soft
crimson.

I Don't Want To Be a Wallflower
(a revision)

Do you like me?
Standing
opaque,
and out of the way—

Taking up space unseen
against
the wall?

Why don't you close in on me,
close enough to
smell my perfume,
please.
Then you'll see
I'm a rose garden—

Pick me,
peel me,
and let me fall
at your feet.

Close in on me,
close enough to
make me
visible.

**Kiss Me
Quickly**

Kiss me
quickly,
        quickly.

Before you
remember
where you
found me.

**But Pain
Is Faceless in the Stoic**

Ravel,
unravel,
ravel…

Travel round-stuck-about;
but pain
is faceless in the stoic.

You
built the road she
travels,
ravels,
unravels…

She
will paint her face
in rage,
enraged
at last
with
your

Infidelity.

Infidel,
you've made a grievous error;
for you may not enter temple,
yet
refuse to pray at altar.

And so,
she will
build new roads
to those where you are
unwelcome

While you ravel,
unravel,
ravel…

Travel round-stuck-about.

**I'm So Fucking Cold
That I Can't Feel It
Anymore**

You don't know what love is at noon o'clock on
Tuesday, when I tell you I'm so cold that I can't even
fucking feel it
anymore, expect for
inside—just inside the doorway where
my walls still quake with a singular mind
not mine, but theirs.

And you can't tell the difference,
like my stupid cunt
can't tell the
difference—the
goddamned
difference 'tween
pleasure and affection.

Noon-thirty,
you gotta get home cos she is waiting cos
your home is her home,
too—
I got no type of home worth
mentioning.

My home shoulda been
your home,
too,
but you got lost—
accident on
purpose.

I don't know what love is at midnight o'clock on
Wednesday, when I answer your call—
I'm so fucking cold
that I can't feel it
anymore.

**Mustard
Potato Salad
and
Pastrami**

Saw your
ashtray face
today
at the supermarket;
you
watched me under the counter
and over the
mustard
potato salad.

Oh!
How far you've come.

I should say thanks
for spitting
down my throat.

Yes,
thanks for the lies,
sugar.
Nothing
kills truer
than nicotine
scented venom.

You never did have the intention
of making me an
honest woman.

It's been years,
but still you burn me.
My reputation smolders,
and I can see the smoke that
billows in their eyes.

I've been forgiven,
but not forgotten.

I hate you,
but I'll take a half pound of your pastrami.

**G.I.
Distress**

Don't be stoopid. It's not me—
definitely you.

1.

Shush, now.

I know
break-ups are rough. Tough like
Rawhide.

Ever watch a dog chew on processed cow skin?
That shit's indigestible; causes intestinal
swelling and diarrhea, etcetera.

Funny,
some relationships are (un)just
oversized break-ups in-waiting,
glazed with meat flavoring for optimal taste.

2.

I used to lounge with you
outside in the summer dark.
Under the stars,
we'd swig bottles of Miller Lite
and inhale Marlboro tobacco;
two Alphas trying
to cancel each other out.

3.

Shush.

That's a goddamned lie.
I
never had int'rest
in your use-less
competition.

Now you howl by yourself,
wondering
who will clean up your vomit.

It's not me—
definitely you.

Sagittarius
Aiming At Antares
(a revision)

Magnificent
weapon,

Sure-shot killer,

My bow and
arrow

See
Lambda,
Delta,
Epsilon,

And Gamma² Sagittarii,
orange

Brighter than the sun—

Tip of my
arrowhead,
vengeful,
does burn

Chase you
'cross the Heavens,

Aiming at Antares

Oh, you

poor
Scorpion
heart

I don't
mean to do it;

It's all written in the stars

**For
All the Pretty Boys
I've Loved**

In consequence of
grand
transgressions,
bodies bob in
putrid
tinted
water.

I captained fastest motor boats
that ran on sweat and
seminal fluids.

I did not burn down
bridges,
rather,
I set fire
to marital mattresses;
and
then
we all
choked on
ashes.

Yes, I captained
fastest motor
boats that ran on sweat and
seminal
fluids—
tapped the bodies,

tossed 'em back,
collected more
to feed my whore
heart.

And I'm sorry for
all the pretty boys
I've loved
and left in
my epic wake.

Shit Happens When You're Trying To Find Yourself

I broke him.
And so I'd broken
me (temporarily).

#sorrynotsorry

part VI
on Love-Love

**For My
Favorite Husband**

Ours
isn't star-crossed.

We are the authors
of this mad
love,
babe.

**In
Rapture**

Resplendent are you,
dressed in Love—
your Sunday
Best

Bare naked
at noon
white teeth flashing,
blue eyes, too

In rapture, in rapture

Oh

Breathing At Midnight

My walls quake in the
breeze of his breathing
at midnight, and I

Inhale in short gasps,
the heartspeak released from his
lips in deep blue gusts.

He Calls Me Beautiful

Like it's my God-given name.

I Have To Remind Myself

Daily to live for the
day,

Cos I find myself
often

Grieving
first morning
I'll wake up
without him.

**We're Not Romantic
In Obvious
Ways**

We're unaffected,
and the best of
friends.
We laugh like children—

Carry on like
no one's watching.
       (everyone is watching)

You buy me Blue Moon
beer and Snickers
ice-cream for my
birthday.

I buy you
comic books.

We're not romantic
in obvious
ways.

You take me to Taco
Bell every Sunday,
and buy me
Haribo Gold
Bears from Wal-Mart
for 98 cents per
5 oz. package.
They're a penny more at Walgreens.

We don't hold hands
in public places
unless
we're goofing,
or it's crowded,
and you
don't want to
lose me.

We don't make out
during movies.
      (at the theater)

We're not romantic
in obvious
ways,
and you
may not always
understand me,
but
you always do
respect me.

I've never respected
a man as much as
I respect you.
      (except for my dad, and Gordon Ramsay)

We're not romantic
in obvious
ways,
but we do carry on like
no one's watching.

My Heart Breaks When I Think of Our End

You're the one
I want to look for
at the end of
breath
and sight,
as we know it
in this life.

part VII
on My Ever Changing State of Mind

**Never
Enough Ice**

Fridge making click sound.
Don't you die, motherfucker.
Need ice for whiskey.
Need whiskey for words, and words
in order to live this life.

**Where Do
My Words Live?**

At the bottom
of a bottle
on a Saturday night.

Sepia

I get drunk on sepia grain
bitter, sweet
memories
breathing
photographs
heaving
bitter, sweet
I get drunk on sepia grain

Monkeys On My Back

It *is* my circus,
and those are my monkeys,
stacked up high—
one and ninety-nine,

Shredding down the big top and feeding me the pieces.

Drama Queen

Of explosive mourning is born the night,
rising low in my rib cage.
Obsidian heart cooling in its crate,
cold enough to freeze the devils in
Hell.
Usurp the king's wings, crow black and cruel;
this is my coronation day.

I've got worms in my veins,
fertilizing melancholy.
Holy blood boils
over
bone and sinew.

See what shit that love has left me.

No More Does Death Do

Sarcophagus closet kept
closed
at the end
of the hall-
way.

Skeleton
key
hangs unused;

A loosened
noose
around my neck
reminds me
that

No more does death
do.

No more does death
do.

No more
does death do
than I have grown accustomed to.

And I can live without you,
here,

On the opposite side

of this closet
door—

Outside of the goddamned closet,
made into your
coffin.

Cold to the Bone

Lungs of disparities
breathe in
unison
gusts.

*I am
disproportionate,*

Speak my voices of
dissidence
in devilish
tongues.

I am the sick in my
own mouth of
madness, and

Cold to the
bone.

I am the moonfaced
ghoul that
lives
beneath
the firmament

And
above ground,
too—

Hell
won't even
host me.

*Because I'm
disproportionate,*

My many demon
voices
speak.

**Brightly
Dark**

Remnants
pulsate, still

Life is art, imitating
dreams built by clay

How cruel the universe, taunting

Rocket
Shipwrecked

Cleanse me
in stardust,
and I might apprehend love,

Cosmically;

For I've been shipwrecked,
cataclysmically—

Marooned
inside of
mine.

Disturb Me, Please

Gimme goddamn
good
reason to

Feel like this
fevered pitchfork

Tongue
tangled
up with
sense my teeth are
trying to speak.

Disturb
me, please—

Gimme goddamn
good
reason to

Receive these
melancholic spiders;

Mean motherfuckers with
frolicking legs that
            (tap-tap-tap)
rap on the latch at
the base of my skull,
and

Whisper hateful
shit
to me in ticklish
silken
tendrils.

Disturb
me, please.

I need goddamn
good
reason.

**For Only
Me**
(a revision)

Every day
it does reign,
a
perpetual
decrescendo—

Melancholic
melody
made
for only
me.

Deluge
of disquiet
comprises
choral pessimists
repeating
in
my
head.

Dirges
designed
for only
me.

And
depressionist
percussionist

beats a heart
that's not yet
dead.

Not yet
dead,

My heart belongs
to only
me.

The Bellows Come Loudest in Daylight

The bellows
come
loudest in
daylight,

Now
that I've captured
the rhythms
of night

Inside
my rib cage.

I keep my heart
in the back
of
my
mouth
now,

And I
can
taste
terrific
arrhythmia

Soon
as the sun

breaks black
into blue.

Trust,
I'll arrest
these daylight
bellows,
too.

I Am Woman

Stay the blade lodged in my back—
let the tissue heal and seal the
covenant.

I am Woman,
unrecumbent,
and daggers only steel
my skin.

Vapor

And I will knot you 'round
my heart—

My anchor
in the
vapor.

Talking to Myself

I bring you
down
to levels unbecoming,
because

I need you to see
the parts
of me
refusing
to be buried.

I am not the dark,
no more than I
am not the sun.

Am I
not
worthy
to wear the name,
Poet?

Am I
not
Inspiration?

Have I
not freed you
from self-
flagellation?

I bring you
down to
levels unbecoming,
because

I know you can
build
monuments from earthworms.

**All the
Beginnings
of
Everything**

I want to be the light at the very beginning,
when shadows steal away,
but still
remain in waiting.

>I want to be the
>dawn
>of
>man,
>beneath the sun,
>and
>in the sand.

>I want to be the
>first taste of
>blood,
>first fire,
>first ice-age,
>and the
>first
>flood.

>I want to be
>Mother
>of lunar eclipse,
>of black holes
>and comets.

End
of words
freed
from your lips.

Last kiss.

Final breath.

I want to be the dark at the very beginning,
when lights fade away,
but still
remain in waiting.

I want to be

All the
beginnings
of
everything.

About the Author

Kindra M. Austin is an author, editor, and micro-publisher from Chesaning, Michigan, USA. Her debut novel was published in April, 2017. To date, Austin has published two poetry books (*Constant Muses*, and *TWELVE*, rated five stars by Readers' Favorite), a novel (*Magpie in August*), and one novella (*For You, Rowena*). She is currently working on a second novel (*Royce with the Rose Gold Hair*) to be released in early 2020.

Other publications include several poems featured on SpillWords; contributions to *Sudden Denouement Anthology Volume I*, *Swear to Me*, and *All the Lonely People*; and four essays and articles advocating for LGBTQ rights, printed in the Ohio Mansfield Pride magazine. She also contributed to, and served as one of four editors for *We Will Not Be Silenced: The Lived Experience of Sexual Harassment and Sexual Assault Told Powerfully Through Poetry, Essay, and Art*.

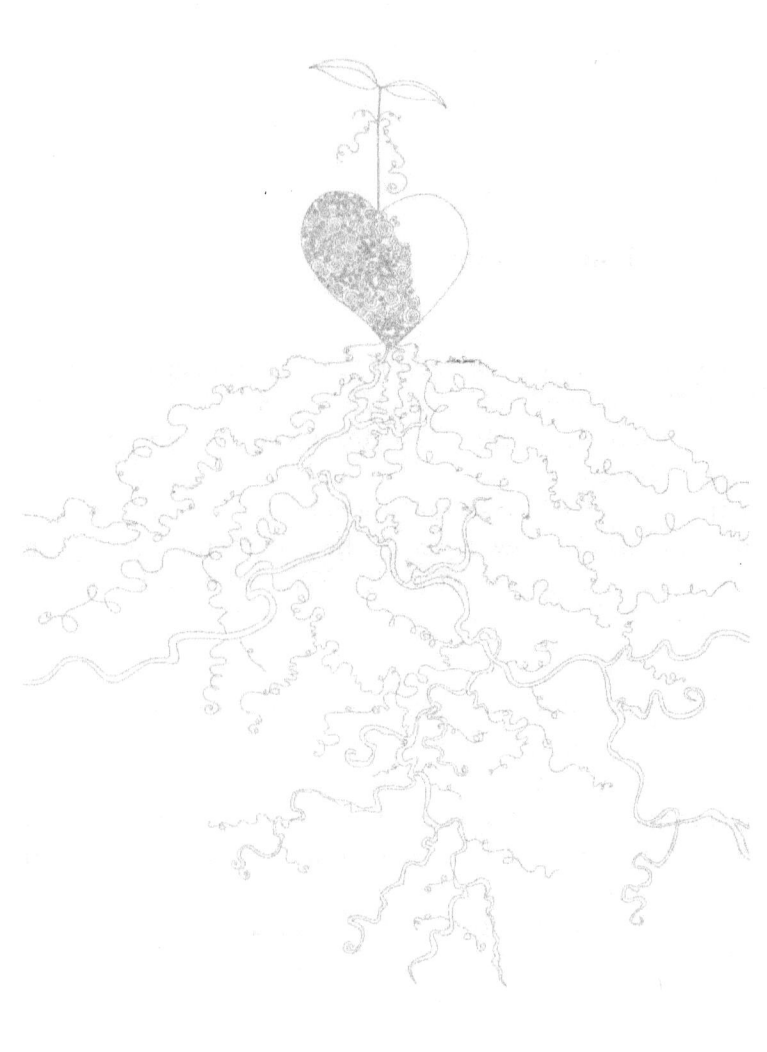

New Novel from Kindra M. Austin

Coming in 2020

Royce
with the
Rose Gold Hair

follow me to read an excerpt

1
Nighttime for Hamady

Hamady: Red Oak County Seat

Hill Gates

It's only Jess, snuck out again to meet her boyfriend.
But there's something vexing about a steady creaking of taut rope rubbing against the bark of a sturdy limb; and when the ceaseless sound springs through nighttime breezes at twelve in the morning, it's downright unnerving.
What if her daddy hears, too?
Millie was quite fond of her young neighbor, Jessica May. She'd often caught the girl with Kyle Lubbock underneath the branches of the biggest oak, squarely squatting in the center of the grove. Jess's father was an awful mean man, and Millie was a nosy-body who did whatever she could to help keep Clipper Simon's belt far away from his only daughter's backside.
Such a stupid girl. Stupid in love, I guess.
Millie abandoned the bed she shared with her husband, and slipped her bare feet into a pair of dingy moccasins. "I'll be back shortly."
Robert rolled over and yawned. "Sweetheart, maybe that girl deserves for her daddy to find out. Not your job to babysit, just sayin."
"Please, Robby. You know what would happen to Jess. I can't stand the thought." She visibly shuddered and released a muted gasp.

"Hell, Mills." He flung off the bed covers with an endearing huff. "Want me to go with you?"

"No, you go back to sleep. I'll take Shamrock. She likes the late night air." Then she let out a whistle. "C'mon, girl. We're goin for a walk."

Millie Williams and the Doberman-Shepherd marched out onto the lamp-lit street, crossed the cul-de-sac, and then quick-stepped through Hill Grove, guided by slivers of moonlight and a pocket-sized flashlight. The creaking grew louder and sharper, causing the woman to internally cringe. Shamrock, however, wasn't bothered by the sound, and she remained focused on the voices that escaped her companion's distracted ears.

"I knew it, Shammy." Millie breathed in deeply, and exhaled her relief. "But wait." She stopped a moment and watched Jessica Simon swing on the tire, alone. "She's cryin somethin terrible. Something's happened."

Maybe she and Kyle had a quarrel.

Shamrock spoke low, but Millie didn't pay attention.

"C'mon, Shammy." She took one step forward, but the dog refused to obey. "Do I need to start leashing you? Would you like that? To be dragged along? Come."

Shamrock stood her ground, and she peeled back her dark, serrated lips.

Millie misinterpreted the warning, and as she opened her scolding mouth wider, something blunt landed hard upon her head. A wrathful howl erupted from an ageless pit, and it was the last voice Millie heard before entering blackness.

* * *

Layers of tape were wrapped crudely around the base of Millie's neck, and covered her mouth. Zip-ties were fastened around her wrists and ankles so tightly that the sharp edged plastic perforated her skin. Her wounded head lay boulder heavy in Jessica's blood blemished lap.

She blinked her screaming eyes.

Where's Shammy? Maybe she's gone for Robby.

Pale grey irises darted, refusing to settle on the girl's screwed-up face.

"I'm sorry, Millie," Jessica wept. "My daddy made me do it. He made me get you to come out here."

Millie willed her body to heave, and she rolled free from the quaking lap. She kept on rolling, inching, and slithering away from the salty wet pleas.

"Please, forgive me. Please." Jessica kept on begging, even as her awful mean daddy stalked Millie, chiding, and waving a pillowcase.

"No law greater than the Lord's," Clipper preached. "I'm only tryin to uphold that law, Millie Hamady-Williams. Never mind that I'm an earth-bound lawman, this is my duty as a God fearin man. We've been tryin and tryin to get rid of your lot, and by God, we will."

Millie visibly shuddered, but could not gasp.

* * *

There's something sinister about the sound of taut rope rubbing against the bark of a sturdy limb; and when the ceaseless sound springs through nighttime breezes in the dark of morning, it's a threat of things to come.

www.ingramcontent.com/pod-product-compliance
Lightning Source LLC
Chambersburg PA
CBHW020416080526
44584CB00014B/1359